Gallery of Western Paintings

Edited by
RAYMOND CARLSON

McGraw-Hill Book Company, Inc.
New York   London   Toronto

For Dad

GALLERY OF WESTERN PAINTINGS

Copyright, 1951, by Hobson & Herr, Inc.

Printed in the United States of America

First Edition

Contents

Foreword

The expression "out where the West begins" is common coin in the language of the realm. I am led to ask, when I hear the phrase, "Just where does the West begin?" It reminds me of another weather-beaten saw: Texans are tall, thin, taciturn. I know Texans who are short, fat and as garrulous as tipsy magpies.

The West definitely does not begin out where they wear big hats and high-heeled boots; nor should all strange beings so attired be considered Westerners. There are many of us who have lived in Arizona all of our lives but have never worn high-heeled boots for the sound and logical reasons that they hurt our feet and we seldom ride horses.

It is more than a matter of geography. A Kansas farmer and an Oklahoma oilman may consider themselves truly of the West, while we who live in Arizona would consider them effete Easterners. That Pandemonium of the Pacific, Los Angeles, can not be considered a Western town, although some *Angelenos* are most typically Western in manner and attitude. Las Vegas, Nevada, that extravaganza in chrome and neon dedicated to the Goddess of Chance, cannot be considered worthy of the adjective any longer, while Pioche, a few miles up the road, is Western right down to its friendly core. No, it is not a matter of geography. West is somewhere between Wilshire Boulevard, the Golden Nugget Saloon, and Wayside, Kansas.

There is a West, though. The makers of movie magic have depended on watered versions of its theme to bolster sagging bank accounts ever since movies were invented. Where the plains break off and the land gets rough and unruly, that's where you find the West. It is a lonely land not gentled by the plow. It is distance spanned but not yet fettered by ribbons of steel and asphalt. It is bigness scarred only by the wind and weather, full of sun and silence, and peace. It is serenity drenched in extravagant colors. This is the West the artists in *Gallery of Western Paintings* have endeavored to interpret. Its natural beauty demands extraordinary talents of its interpreters, talents which these nine artists very definitely share.

RAYMOND CARLSON

Ross Santee

Ross Santee writes books and draws pictures for a living. Consider *Cowboy, Men and Horses, The Bubbling Spring,* and *Apacheland* among others. They are good books, devoid of frill and frippery, written the same way Ross draws a picture. Like his books, his pictures tell a story, simply and honestly, and by these virtues attain their strength and vigor.

He was born in Thornburg, Iowa, August 16, 1889. He was raised in Iowa and Illinois, and studied at the Chicago Art Institute. Like so many artists before and after, he went to New York to win fame and fortune, but both seemed to elude him at the same time that their blessings were lavishly heaped on his friends. He knew confusion and discouragement. He took advice from everyone and became more confused than ever. (Later he had much to say about advice. In fact he wrote an article about it for a national magazine: "Advice Is All Right If You Don't Take Too Much of It.") He tried to draw cartoons, but what he drew turned out to be imitations of cartoons drawn better by others. A turning point in his life came when his friend, artist Thomas Benton, gave him a book of drawings by Daumier. "It was that book of drawings by Daumier," he says, "that made up my mind for me, for he put things down just like he saw or felt the thing, without the sign of a trick." He resolved that if he ever drew again he would draw just what he felt and saw.

He felt the strong urge to draw again when he was a horse wrangler for a big spread in Gila County, Arizona, a short time later. That was in 1915. The horses, the cattle drive, the lonely rider on the mesa, the dust of the corral, the shine of saddle leather, the hills burnt brown by the sun—these were the scenes he yearned to sketch honestly, and "without tricks." He heard endless stories around campfires and what he heard he remembered and later included in magazine pieces and in books. One such story, "Water," was published in *Collier's* and won for him an O. Henry award in 1935. It has been reprinted in several anthologies and is a fine piece of writing. Yet it is no more dramatic than the drawing that went with it, which, in a few simple lines, depicted the terror and cruelty of drought.

The panorama of the range passed before him during those years he was a horse wrangler (he says he never was good enough to be called a cowboy), and he himself became a part of that panorama. He liked what he saw, and he drew it the way he saw it and the way he felt about it. Fortunately, editors liked his drawings. When he wrote stories and made drawings for his own stories, editors liked them, too.

When he left the Western range, he took part of the range with him. It is with him today, reflected in his personality and his appearance, in his books and drawings.

Santee lives in Arden, Delaware, but he spends much time in the West.

Sketches by Santee appear on type pages throughout this book.

Charles M. Russell

Charlie Russell rode with the best of them, drank with the best of them, painted with the best of them. An epoch of the West that is gone now—the West before the plow came to turn over the grass, before the snorting iron horse came to frighten the buffalo herds and pollute the air, before barbed wire was put up to choke off the endless acres—that is the epoch of the West Charlie Russell knew and loved and painted so vividly and faithfully that it will live for us always as part of our great frontier heritage.

Charles Marion Russell was born in St. Louis in the turbulent year 1864. To the east and south, like a stifling mantle over the land, lay the smoke and bitterness of civil war. To the west was the bright land of promise, unknown mountains to be climbed, rough trails to be ridden, rivers with strange names beckoning to the strong and venturesome. Through the St. Louis of Charlie Russell's boyhood days passed a long cavalcade of pioneers and adventurers seeking the new land. Charlie wanted to tag along.

As a boy he had two outstanding characteristics—great natural artistic ability, which his mother encouraged, and an impelling desire to go West to the land he had heard so much about from traders, trappers, and frontiersmen—a desire his father labored mightily to discourage, but to no avail.

His "book learning" was limited, simply because he would not stay in school. His formal art education consisted of three restless days in an art class. After all, how could he get interested in drawing a plaster foot? His

dreams were far beyond the wide rivers, where trail herds were being driven, where the endless prairie was the domain of proud Indian tribes, and where the silence of the land was broken only by the hoofs of buffalo on the run. The boy's dreams came true. The elder Russell finally relented and in March, 1880, at the age of sixteen, Charlie was on his way West.

The Montana Territory in the eighties was a land guaranteed to excite any lad in his teens so long as he had an eye for adventure and a skin thick enough to stand rough treatment and all kinds of weather. There lived the Piegan and the Crow, the Blackfoot and the Flathead Indians, proud and colorful tribes whose progeny, years later, were to be humiliated in overcrowded reservations. The trapper and the plainsman, before civilization made them extinct species, were stimulating companions, especially for a boy of sixteen; and the land itself—the bigness and the color of it—could hardly fail to provoke artistic responses in the young Russell.

His knowledge of the West was acquired the hard way; he became a cowpuncher, and one worthy of his keep. Although always an artist, he was far from a mere observer. He became part of the vanishing frontier, a gay, friendly, rollicking figure with a sensitive eye for the pageant of history swirling around him. Wherever he rode, there was a box of water colors and a sketch pad in his bedroll. He was always making sketches of what he saw, or molding figures out of clay, or whittling. His sensitive artist's hands were always busy.

(Text Continued on Page 15)

6

N WAGON TRAILS WERE DIM

WHEN THE TRAIL WAS LONG BETWEEN CAMPS

TIGHT DALLY AND LOOSE LATIGO

WAITING FOR A CHINOOK

CM Russell

The Last of 5

THE CHALLENGE

AT THE END OF THE ROPE

RETURN OF THE WARRIORS

Charlie Russell's early pictures were traded over bars for drinks for himself and his friends. His first studio was in the back room of a saloon in Great Falls, Montana. The public first saw his paintings on saloon walls, where his barkeep friends were glad to hang them. He was proud to have them shown there, too, because they met the approval of a most critical audience—his fellow cowpunchers. He painted and made drawings for the fun of it, caring little what he received for them.

His beloved wife Nancy, whom he married in September, 1896, changed his attitude considerably. She became business manager in the Russell household and studio in Great Falls, and she taught Charlie to consider himself seriously as an artist. No longer were Russell paintings passed across bars in return for drinks. Nancy believed implicitly in the value of her husband's work and she insisted on good prices. Usually she got them. With marriage and the obligations that go with it, Charlie's carefree days were over. He had a wife to support and a household to maintain. He had to paint now, not just for fun, but for a livelihood. His young wife, by attending to the business end of the artist's life, saved him from the part of it he liked the least.

"After we was married," Russell once told a friend, "Nancy set about to change me, an' she shore did. Bill Rogers said, 'She took one of the 'o's outa saloon an' made it salon'.'"

"The lady I trotted in double harness with," he said on another occasion, "was the best booster an' pardner a man ever had. She could convince anybody that I was the greatest artist in the world, an' that makes a feller work harder. You just can't disappoint a person like that, so I done my best work for her."

In his lifetime, and to his great surprise, he saw some of his paintings sold for sums up in the five figures. Few artists have lived to see such success and fame, with their attendant rewards, as came to Charlie Russell during the last decades of his life. Too often an artist's contemporaries fail to appreciate his efforts and leave such discrimination to future generations. It was not so with Charles Marion Russell.

He is dead now, but his work has a permanent place in the annals of American art. His paintings and his bronzes are cherished items in our greatest museums and in private collections. He will live, as well, in the stories they tell around campfires as long as there are cattle on the ranges and men to drive them. In the West it is felt that he was more than just an artist. Because he was so much a part of the scene he portrayed on canvas, he endeared himself to whole generations of ranch hands, plainsmen, and pioneers. His friends were legion, for he was gay, witty, and wild in his youth, a kindly, sagacious man in his maturity.

At a time when few people even gave them a passing thought, Russell was a champion of the Indians. He knew and appreciated their problem and had a deep understanding of the red man's religion and philosophy. "I've known some bad Injuns," he once said, "but for every bad one I kin match 'im with ten worse white men."

The story of this American artist is well told by Ramon Adams and Homer E. Britzman in their *Charles M. Russell—A Biography*. They recount that shortly before his death October 24, 1926, in Great Falls, realizing he would soon die, he said, "I want to be carried to the grounds behind hosses." His wish was honored. A horse-drawn hearse was found and Charlie Russell went out "behind hosses."

15

William R. Leigh

The life of William Robinson Leigh is a life dedicated to art. Now, in his golden decades (he was born in 1866), it is pleasing to note that in early 1951 a showing of his water colors in New York was one of the most successful shows he has ever had. The years have not dimmed his love and understanding of the Western scene; nor have they lessened the artistry of his brush. A tall, distinguished gentleman, with all the grace and manners of an old Southern planter, he has accepted time's frowns and favors with dignity, remaining true to his mission as an artist, formulated many years ago, of translating the beauty and grandeur of the West into pigment on canvas.

Leigh was born in Virginia. Of his childhood he writes: "When I was a small child in Virginia, we had a buffalo (bison) pelt in our house—as almost everybody did in those days. I wallowed and rolled on that soft robe that lay on the floor, but not without my imagination being stirred. In our Cassell's *Popular Natural History* there was a woodcut of bison, the sun was rising behind a big butte, and water was in the foreground. But the bison was rather small and inexact.

"I knew the names of most of the animals of the world before I could read, and I listened to my mother breathlessly as she read the writings of Sir Samuel Baker, Livingston, Stanley; I cut out of paper stirring compositions, and drew dramatic animal scenes on my slate. On one of my cuttings—an elephant chasing a man on horseback—I won first prize at the Martinsburg County Fair—one dollar. And then, one day my father read the account of the Custer Massacre from the newspaper. This was in 1876, when I was ten years old; it made a tremendous impression on me."

Years later his painting "Custer's Last Fight" was acquired by the Woolaroc Museum in Oklahoma, where it hangs today, an outstanding painting in a great collection.

He was sent to the Maryland Institute in Baltimore where he worked for three years. Then, in 1883 he went to Munich to study in the Royal Academy. For twelve years he literally submerged himself in the art of Europe. There he learned to draw and paint; there he also became convinced that the subject matter that interested him most was the young, vigorous land across the Atlantic, his native America.

He returned home in the mid-nineties. That was the gay, mauve decade, a pleasant, placid time for our country, but an era when Americans were, perhaps more than ever before or after, enslaved by European culture. Americans knew that they were barbarians, because they paid good money to hear European lecturers tell them so. The fountain of wealth that was America was turning out droves of millionaires, who, in turn, were turning out comely daughters whose main function in life was to get themselves married to titled young men from abroad. The

(Text Continued on Page 25)

16

COMBING THE RIDGES

THE FEMALE OF THE SPECIES

BAKING DAY

THE MYSTIC

W. R. Leigh. 1910.

THE RESCUE

HOME SWEET HOME

THE VOICE OF THE DESERT

millionaires, the comely daughters, and the titled husbands built costly palaces that were, in many cases, dehydrated imitations of more costly palaces elsewhere. The only conceivable art that could be used to decorate such mansions had to be the work of European artists with unpronounceable names. Young American artists like William Leigh did not qualify.

Art dealers—and how important a sympathetic art dealer can be in the career of a young artist—were disinterested. Paint America? There was nothing in America worth painting! The West? Full of dirty Indians and drunken cowboys! Preposterous!

William Leigh, a desperately serious young artist, met rebuff after rebuff; yet he never faltered in his belief that he would find a place for himself in American art and that he would win that place by painting the subjects he wanted to paint. He managed to make a living as best he could. He worked for *Scribner's* as an illustrator, and by 1906, at long last, he had saved enough money to take his first trip West. Destination, Laguna, New Mexico!

The storied land that he had always dreamed about did not disappoint him. He traveled widely through the territories of New Mexico and Arizona, absorbing the color of the land, visiting the pueblos, and making sketch after sketch to guide him later in his paintings. On this study trip he realized how right he had been in his desire to know and paint America.

"I saw Acoma and the Grand Canyon," he has written. "I knew that some of the most distinctive, characteristic, dramatic, poetic, unique motifs in the world were here in this virgin country waiting an adequate hand to do them justice. Thereafter, I was in the West as often as I could earn enough money to take me there."

His fellow artists, who had not seen the West, laughed at his paintings. The color, they said, was ridiculously false, and his pictures nothing but "illustrations." Everything he did was so labeled until he produced "The Poisoned Pool." Recognition came slowly but surely. His paintings began to command better prices and were gradually being sought by discriminating buyers and museums. Among his patrons today are the Duke of Windsor and the King of Belgium.

Leigh was the painter chosen to accompany the Carl Akeley Expedition to East Africa for the American Museum of Natural History, 1926-1927, and the museum's Carlisle-Clark Expedition to the same locality in 1928. During the period 1932-1935 he had charge of the painting of African landscape backgrounds for habitat groups in the Carl Akeley African Hall in the American Museum of Natural History. His book *Frontiers of Enchantment*, which appeared in 1938, is a dramatic account of his adventures as an artist in Africa. His keen love of animals, which he exhibited from earliest childhood, has remained with him throughout the years.

The success and recognition that has come to William Leigh has been richly deserved. His enthusiasm for the West has never waned. He has long since proven his point that America and the West are worthy subjects for art.

25

Gray Bartlett

Death stilled the brush of Gray Bartlett in late July, 1951. He was stricken by a heart attack at his studio in Los Angeles just as he was achieving a secure place in American art.

The artist was born July 3, 1885, in Rochester, Minnesota, but when he was very young the family moved to Colorado, fabulous land of high mountains, deep canyons, racing rivers, and endless distance.

Almost before he was big enough to hold a pencil he was trying to draw, but when he became a cowboy at the age of sixteen—how many millions of starry-eyed boys before and since have dreamed of being a cowboy at the age of sixteen—the artistic temperament that lived in Gray Bartlett became a dominant influence in his life. He knew the open range, the solitude of lonely places, the glory and silence of nights alone under Western skies. He was profoundly moved by the freedom, spaciousness, and beauty in which he found himself; he tried to capture these deep feelings in the sketchbook which he always carried.

At first his ambition was to be a rancher, for the wide, open life in the West seemed to suit him so well. Then he began to realize how strongly he felt about his sketches and paintings of Western scenes. Eventually he knew for a certainty that he wanted to be an artist. He first studied art at the Greeley Art School and then by virtue of a scholarship entered the Chicago Art Institute. He worked at various odd jobs to support himself while in school, but his formal training in the field of art was cut short by the illness and death of his mother. He was forced to give up his art studies and find work in Colorado to help support the family.

The practical responsibilities of life—marrying, raising a family, earning a living—did not allow Gray Bartlett to return to his sketch pad and canvas for thirty years. He became a commercial artist, employed by various photo-engraving companies. Job followed job in rapid succession in Denver, Davenport, Minneapolis, and other cities of the West and Middle West. Eventually he married, and then on $1,800 borrowed capital he purchased an interest in an engraving firm. Over the years his business prospered, and in 1937 he was able to retire and move to California.

There, after an interval of thirty years in which he had achieved such outstanding success in the business world, Gray Bartlett resumed his study of art. The old, frayed sketchbook which in his youth he had carried in his saddlebag became once again the center of his life. The Western scenes he had once yearned to paint—mountain ranges, old trails, water holes, dusty sagebrush, sturdy ponies—remained as evocative and beautiful as of old. His desire to paint returned stronger than ever and, although neglected for so many years, his skill with a brush and his eye for color did not fail him.

(Text Continued on Page 35)

26

BART'S PLACE

INDIAN CAMP

Gray Bartlett

THE OX TRAIN

SADDLED FOR THE FIRST TIME

THE NIGHT HERD

The West became his workshop—Arizona, New Mexico, Texas, Colorado, and Utah. He had one studio in California and another near Moab in Utah, one of America's last frontiers. He was also part owner of a cattle ranch in southern Utah, where he spent much of his time renewing associations with a life he thought he had left forever.

Another consuming interest played an important part in his painting. The Indian tribes of the West and Southwest, with all their picturesque, primitive qualities, had great appeal for Bartlett as they do for many other fine artists of the West. He lived among them, made friends with them, and left his tracks broad and wide through their land. He painted them as one who possessed an intimate knowledge of their ways.

Although kept from his lifework for many years by the hard economic facts of life, Gray Bartlett never harbored a regret. He was a pleasant, affable, friendly man, doing just the things he always wanted to do. Neither his talent nor his desire was dimmed by the pressures and cares of thirty years in the business world. His life, and his outstanding success in both fields, cast interesting light on the endless and much-discussed struggle between art and commerce.

"I paint the things I like to paint," Bartlett once wrote, "and in so doing derive great enjoyment and satisfaction from my art. I do not select my subject matter to cater to a particular taste or a particular market. If I did so, I feel I would be doing things which I would not enjoy doing and which would not be a source of inspiration to me. Luckily, the three dealers in the United States who handle all the paintings that I can produce, find ready buyers for my work, so I am content in following my own desires.

"I get my ideas by traveling through the parts of the West I most enjoy to portray and living among the people whose lives I find enjoyment in depicting. While out on these trips I make numerous pencil sketches of anything which I think might be useful in the makeup of a painting. I also take many photographs of people and scenery. Much of the material I get is retained in my memory and when the time comes for the painting to be put on canvas, I do this in my studio. With the help of my sketches, my photographs and with imagination and with memory to beautify the painting, I try to produce not only a beautiful piece of art but an authentic one as well.

"The test of a painting is Truth and Beauty. Truth comes with knowledge, with patience. The artist must learn all details that are the component parts of a landscape, a person or an animal he wishes to portray before he is able to do that well. The search for that knowledge is one of the great pleasures that painting has given me."

Ross Santee
Arizona

35

Frederic Remington

Time has only enhanced the name and fame of Frederic Remington in the field of art. He is considered today one of the greatest artists this country has ever produced. His twenty-four works of Western sculpture, which were cast in bronze, and his paintings and drawings, which numbered about 3,000, are rare treasures of inestimable value in America's great art collections.

He was a writer, a war correspondent, an illustrator, and a dramatist. He never drew or painted a picture or wrote a story that concerned a more interesting personality than himself. Through the fascinating pages of Harold McCracken's *Frederic Remington— Artist of the Old West*, this engaging genius comes to life.

It can be said that Frederic Remington lived a short life but a merry one. He was born in Canton, New York, October 1, 1861. He died December 24, 1909, at his home near Ridgefield, Connecticut, at the age of forty-eight. In between those dates a life was lived that was one of achievement, action, laughter, and adventure.

His father was a prosperous newspaper publisher who had a distinguished career as a colonel of cavalry in the Civil War. On both sides of his family he was descended from early New England Colonial stock. At home Frederic Remington, as a boy, received every advantage; he was encouraged to live exactly the kind of life he wanted to live.

He attended Highland Military Academy at Worcester, Massachusetts, where he decided on his career and whence he wrote to a friend: "I am going to try to get into Cornell College . . . and if I succeed will be a journalist. I mean to study for an artist anyhow, whether I ever make a success of it."

He entered Yale to study art but quickly developed a distaste for formal art education.

At Yale he found something more to his liking: football and prize fighting. He was star "rusher" on the team of 1879, which was captained by one of the immortals of football, Walter Camp. The night before the Yale-Harvard game, Remington dipped his jersey in blood at a slaughterhouse, signifying that he was ready for battle no matter how rough and gory it might be.

At the end of Remington's second year at Yale his father died, leaving him a modest inheritance. A youthful love affair caused the restless and reckless young man to decide to leave college and go West to win his fortune. The girl of his choice returned his love, but her stern parents felt that the young man was too unstable to accept added responsibilities.

He found the rugged life of the West to his liking, glorying in its roughness. It was a pattern of living that fitted his own temperament, in which a person with his high spirits and physical pugnacity could feel at home. It did not take him long to get out of the category of greenhorn; he held his own with the best of the natives in every phase of their outdoor existence and won for himself immediate respect and friendship. Of the East by breeding and background, he soon became entirely wedded to life in the West.

He found something else perhaps even more important than the rough-and-ready life in a young land—the inspiration that was to lead to his career. This is how he described it:

"Evening overtook me one night in Montana . . . with an old wagon freighter who shared his bacon and coffee with me. I was but nineteen years of age. Over the evening pipes it developed that he had gone West at an early age . . . and during his long life he had followed the receding frontier, always further and further. He sadly lamented the coming of civilization and the passing of the

(Text Continued on Page 45)

36

HOLDING UP THE PAYROLL

APACHES LISTENING

AN OLD TIME PLAINS FIGHT

ON THE SOUTHERN PLAINS IN 1860

BRINGING HOME THE NEW COOK

AMONG THE LED HORSES

SNOWBOUND ON THE OVERLAND STAGE

West. I saw men swarming into the land. I knew the derby hat, the smoking chimney, the cord binder and the thirty-day note were upon us in a surge. I knew the wild riders and the vacant land were to vanish forever—and the more I considered the subject, the bigger the *forever* seemed. Without knowing exactly how to do it, I began to try to record some facts around me, and the *more* I looked, the more the panorama unfolded . . ."

He plunged into the life of the West as few artists have done before or since. His biographer, Harold McCracken, describes that life in glowing terms.

"Remington sought out the most exciting spots from Old Mexico to Canada. He traveled the routes of the Santa Fe Trail, the Oregon Trail, and a number of less known trails pioneered by such men as Kit Carson, Jebediah Smith, and others who had led the way to the taming of the West. He wandered from Texas to Montana as a vagabond on horseback, worked some as a hired cowboy; rode with *posses* after renegade Indians where shoot-to-kill was the order-of-the-day; and did some serious prospecting in Arizona Territory in the area where Geronimo and his Apache followers were most active in their favorite occupation of ambush, murder, and massacre. This was six years before Geronimo, the wily Apache leader, gave in to the U. S. Army; and ten years before Sitting Bull, Medicine Chief of the Sioux, was killed on the verge of his biggest uprising."

He attached himself to contingents of United States Cavalry chasing wild Apaches over the unruly landscape. He wandered through Texas and, having money and being carefree by nature, proved a roisterous companion for kindred souls. He lived for several months with the Comanches, where he learned to admire their handling and training of horses.

He rode hard, drank hard, and fought hard in a society where men were highly esteemed for their ability in these arts; but there was always that deep urge within him to record the scenes about him. No one knows how many sketches he sent back to Eastern magazines. *Harper's Weekly* on February 25, 1882, printed his first sketch, entitled "Cowboys of Arizona, drawn by W. A. Rogers from a sketch by Frederic Remington." His original sketch had to be redrawn.

The fortune that he had hoped to make in the West had not materialized, and his inheritance was running out. In an effort to replenish his funds, he first bought a small ranch in Kansas, which immediately became a gay rendezvous for every saddle tramp in the West, and then a third interest in a notorious saloon in Kansas City, which he enlivened by his own robust patronage. But neither venture earned him any money. He was too busy painting and living the wild life to make a success at business.

In 1884 he returned to New York and married the young lady he had always hoped to marry. But he could not make a satisfactory living for himself and his bride in Kansas, and she returned to her home. Remington returned to New York in 1885, down to his last three dollars, but with high resolve to sell the sketches he had been working on so long. The issue of *Harper's Weekly* of January 9, 1886, carried the first Remington picture to be published in a national magazine under his own name. It was the cover picture entitled "The Apache War—Indian Scouts on Geronimo's Trail."

So began the career of the artist Frederic Remington. In his paintings, sketches, and bronzes, the spirit of the Old West has been captured and will be retained forever. They are more than art treasures now. They are historical documents which we can turn to time and again to remind ourselves of those vigorous days when the West was young.

A monument to his genius is the Remington Art Memorial, Ogdensburg, New York, where some of his finest work can be seen.

Maynard Dixon

The distinguished art critic Arthur Millier, in his monograph "Maynard Dixon—Painter of the West," has admirably summed up, in part, the art of Maynard Dixon:

"For more than half a century Maynard Dixon has painted the life and landscape of the American West. In easel paintings and mural decorations, in drawings and illustrations he has epitomized the beauty and grandeur of its vast deserts, towering mountains, awe-inspiring canyons and remote valleys and has recorded the life of its white settlers and the ancient ways of its indigenous red men. Viewed as a whole, his lifework constitutes the first successful attempt to interpret the West pictorially entirely in terms of the region itself.

"Many artists have pictured some aspects of Western land and life. But their viewpoints have too often been limited. Several have celebrated the life of the cattle range and romanticized the exploits of desperadoes. Others have specialized in paintings of grandiose scenery. Dixon has gone deeper than these.

" . . . Peaks, canyons, mesas, and endless deserts under seemingly fathomless blue skies appear in most of his pictures. Cowboys riding lonely trails; Navajos herding sheep in waterless wastes; Hopis in their many-tiered pueblos; the covered wagons, pony express riders, and scouts of pioneer days—he has loved, studied and painted them all, but with a difference. For Dixon has known and seen the Western country as something more than a source of astonishment for tourists, and a background for pictorial horse opera."

Maynard Dixon is gone now. He died in 1946, at the age of seventy-two. During the last decade of his life, death was so near, a hovering shadow over a vibrant, intensely alive personality, as to be almost a good companion; yet during those pain-wracked years he painted such dramatic Southwestern landscapes as "Desert Ranges," "Peace in October," "Lonesome Road," "Drought and Downpour," and "Red Gateway," all reproduced herein. One who might have met him late in his life would first have been moved to pity at the sight of a very sick man. When you looked into his eyes and saw that mischievous glint and then the slightly satiric but still sympathetic smile, you would have forgotten your pity and lost yourself in admiration for a courageous man. May-

(*Text Continued on Page 55*)

46

RED GATEWAY

DROUGHT AND DOWNPOUR

THE WISE MEN

COWBOY AND PACKHORSE

PEACE IN OCTOBER

DESERT RANGES

LONESOME ROAD

KATCHINAMAKER

nard Dixon knew all the joys and happiness that fall to man's lot on earth, and possessed the wisdom that comes of living a full life.

He was born in Fresno, California, in the year 1875. His parents were Virginians, and from them he inherited his impeccable taste. The country in which he was born was a colorful, rough pioneer land, which made lasting impressions upon him. Of frail health as a youth, he was forced by circumstances to depend upon himself for his own amusement, and his pony and his sketchbook became his best companions. His ambition as a boy was to be an artist and his idol was Frederic Remington. At the age of sixteen he sent a group of sketches to Remington and received a friendly and encouraging note in return.

His first job was as a newspaper illustrator in San Francisco. He covered crime and feature stories the way a modern news photographer would do it. This experience gave him a facile draftsmanship and a sure grasp of design. It also contributed greatly to his understanding of people. Could a young artist possibly receive better schooling?

His repute as an illustrator spread to the extent that he was commissioned to do illustra-tions for magazines and books. His work took him to New York for five years, but his love of the West never abated; whenever money and time permitted he took long excursions west of the Mississippi, and his sketchbooks became chronicles that recorded the country from Montana to Mexico, from Idaho to the Golden Gate.

Ultimately he returned to the West Coast, and his home became San Francisco. For forty of his seventy-two years his studio in that gay city was a vital part of its art world. He began to devote less time to his illustrations and more time to his own career as an individual artist, and by 1920 his work was receiving wide critical acclaim.

From the beginning, mural painting played an important part in Dixon's development as an artist. Some of his notable achievements in this field are: Room of the Dons, Mark Hopkins Hotel, San Francisco; Main Reading Room, California State Library; Arizona Biltmore, Phoenix, Arizona; Bureau of Indian Affairs, Department of Interior Building, Washington, D.C.; Post Offices at Martinez, California, and Canoga Park, California; and the City Ticket Office of the Santa Fe Railway in Los Angeles.

Gerard Curtis Delano

Charles Russell once described the Navajos as being "picture-book" people. The artist Gerard Curtis Delano has found them so, too, and it is significant to note that much of his reputation as an artist has come from the truly fine work he has done on this subject.

These proud, aristocratic Indians live on a reservation that occupies the largest part of northeastern Arizona, northwestern New Mexico, and a small corner of southeastern Utah. The Navajo tribe is the largest Indian tribe in the United States; of all American Indians, the Navajos have been least affected by the Western movement of civilization. Yet they constitute an economic problem that should be the concern of every American, for in the immensity that is Navajo land there is little arable soil and no industry of importance. There is only sand and slick rock and scarcely enough vegetation to support the wandering herds of sheep that represent the one source of income for these nomads of the desert.

The thoughtless and unobservant tourist hurrying through their domain to reach some town where he will find a cocktail lounge and a hot bath, sees the Navajos as "dirty Indians" and their land as dismal wilderness. But an artist like Delano, in his quest for beauty, sees a great deal more and describes it eloquently.

"Navajo! symbol of dark-skinned mystery, color and romance. Navajo! centaur-like nomads, following their sheep and the seasons across the desert. Nothing gives me more pleasure or greater thrill than seeing in real life the brightly clothed Navajos against their backgrounds of magnificent canyons, or the vast open stretches which are characteristic of their reservation country.

"There is a vastness, an immensity, and the peaceful hush of an enormous cathedral about Arizona's great canyons. Whoever has been within these towering walls, who has seen the flocks of sheep and goats grazed there by the Navajos; who has heard the distant tinkle of the lead goat's bell and listened to the wild and eerie songs of the bright-skirted shepherdesses, and who has seen in the distance an approaching rider—a tiny speck against the massive canyon walls—must yearn to perpetuate his impressions of those precious moments."

Delano was born April 14, 1890, in Marion, Massachusetts, a descendant of the French Huguenot pilgrim, Philippe de Lannoy, who landed at Plymouth from the ship *Fortune* in 1621. He had shown a talent for drawing in his early childhood, a talent that was recognized and encouraged by his parents. He began his art studies at the Swain Free School of Design at New Bedford, Massachusetts. He continued them at the Art Students League of New York, under the famous draftsman, the late George Bridgeman, and the noted painters Frank Vincent Dumond and Edward Dufner. He also studied under illustrators Dean Cornwell, Harvey Dunn, and the late

(Text Continued on Page 65)

VERMILION CLIFFS

SHEEP ON THE DESERT

NAVAJO BOY

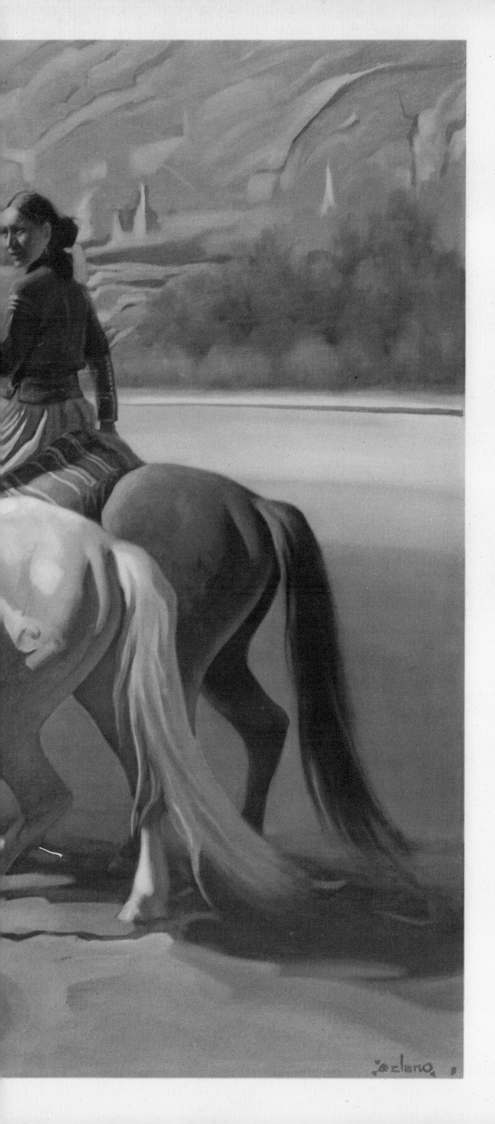

NAVAJO

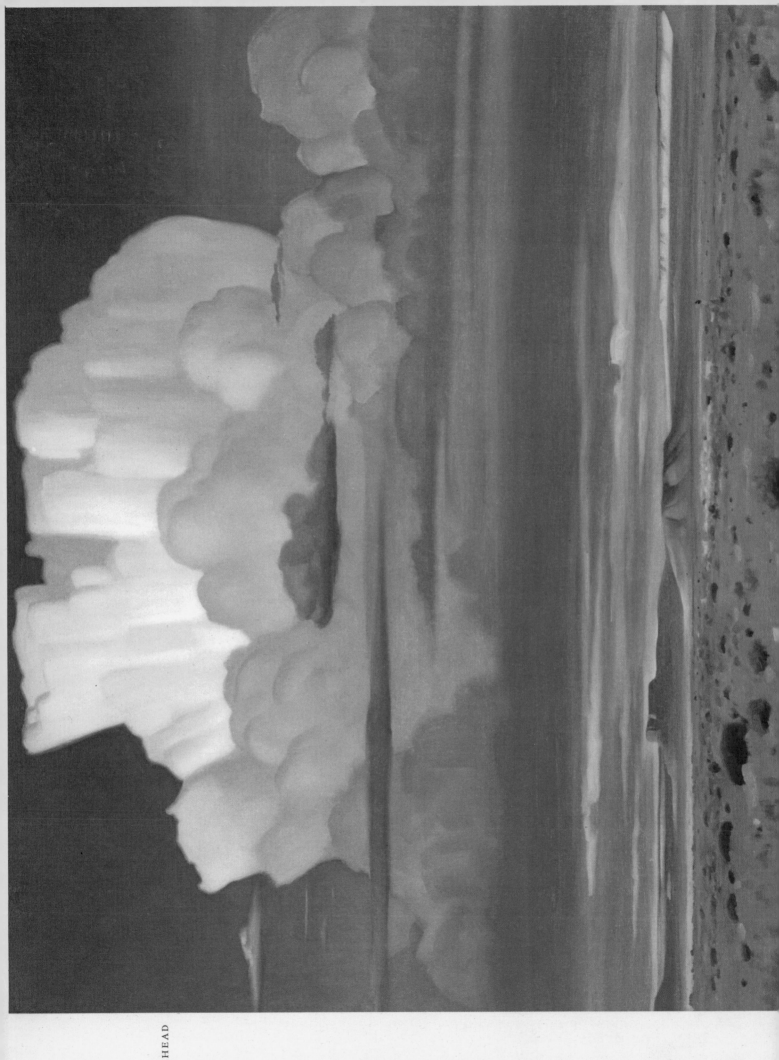

DESERT THUNDERHEAD

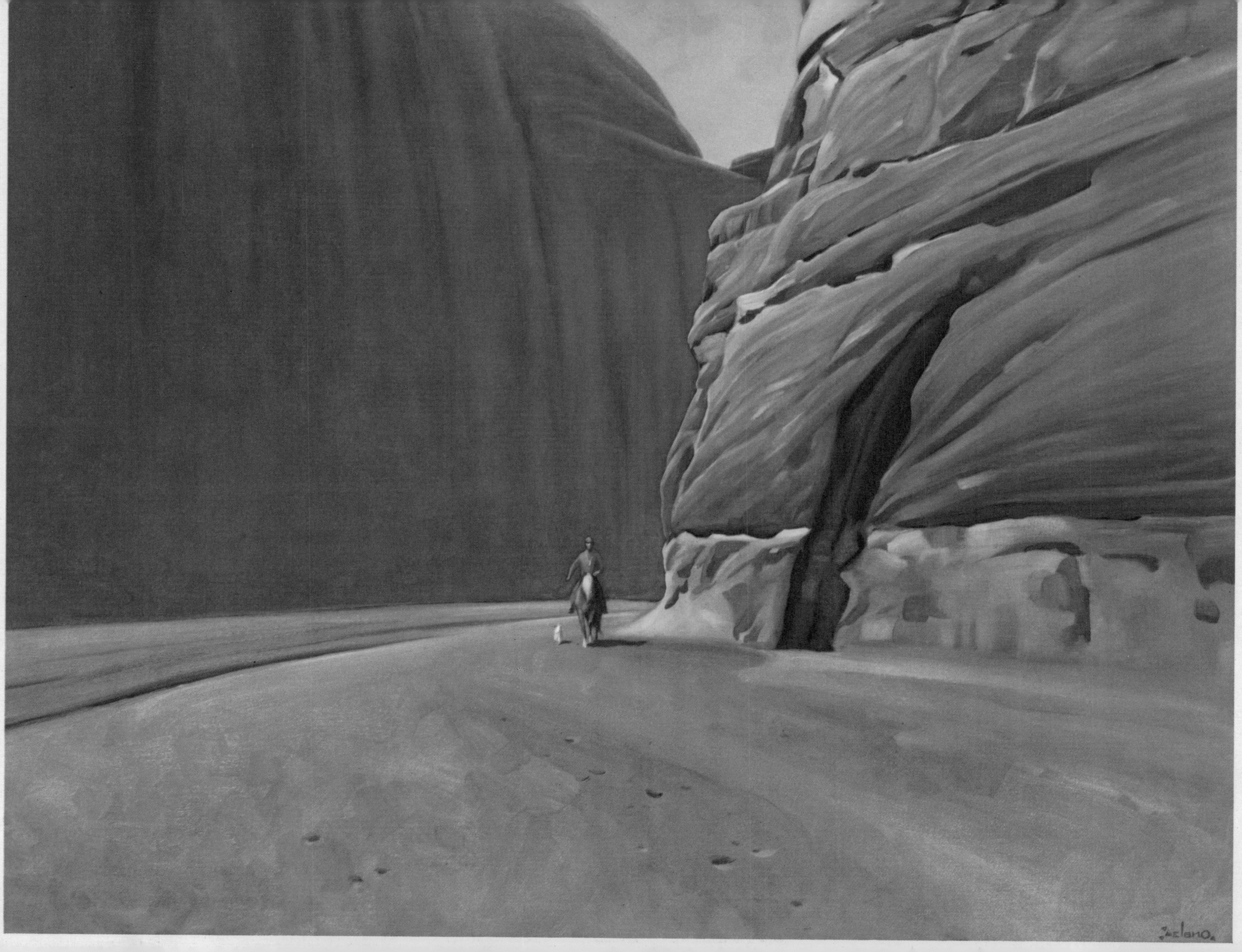

THE CANYON

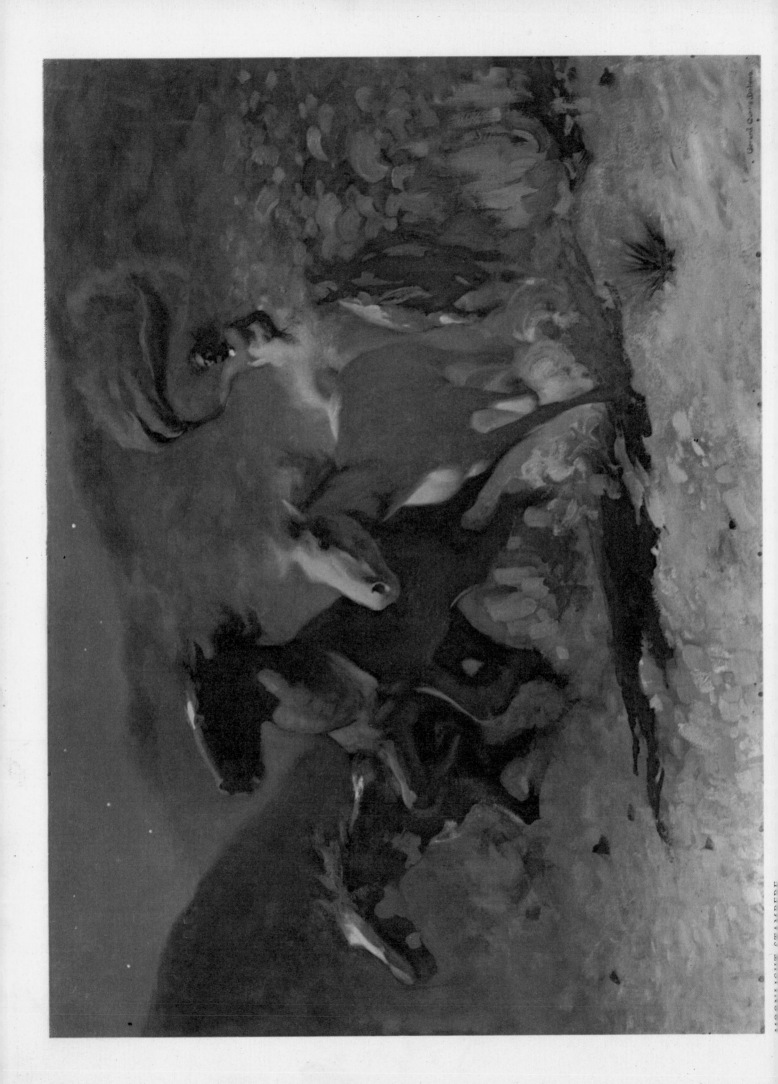

MOONLIGHT STAMPEDE

N. C. Wyeth. Under these able teachers the artist acquired a solid knowledge of art forms which was to serve him in practically every variety of commercial art. His humorous sketches appeared in leading magazines in this country and England. He drew women's fashions, became an animator of movie cartoons, worked as an artist for advertising agencies, painted magazine covers, and was successful as an illustrator. His career in the field of commercial art was a lucrative one, but was interrupted by World War I.

After being mustered out in 1919, he decided to satisfy a lifetime desire to visit the West. From art circles in New York to a cattle ranch in Colorado might be a long jump for some, but Delano managed to bridge the gap. He responded vigorously to life in the West and was deeply moved by the new country in which he found himself. The next year he homesteaded a location on Cataract Creek in Summit County, Colorado, where he built with his own hands a log cabin. He had found the place he was looking for, the place that inspired him as an artist and a place that answered his needs for living.

After "proving" his homestead, he commuted for several years between Colorado and New York. In one place he painted the things he wanted to paint; in the other his talents were for hire on the commercial market. During the depression, Delano decided to move permanently to his mountain cabin, which he did in 1933. He has been a Westerner ever since.

It was not an easy life that he adopted. He was far from the markets where art was sold, and his sales at first were few. His daily routine was difficult. When winter blizzards came to the high mountains of Colorado, it required courage and determination not to give up. Each day he chopped ice from the water hole, cleared the paths of the heavy snow, and kept the fire going in the fireplace. "That artist feller up on Cataract Creek," his neighbors said, "has the makings of a mountain man."

Ultimately fortune rewarded him for his belief in himself and in the land of his choice. A Western-story magazine hired him to do "The Story of the West," a weekly feature with drawings and text that was to be a complete presentation of the development of the Western frontier from the beginning of the nineteenth century to modern times. In his search for authentic detail Delano haunted the larger libraries of Colorado, interviewed hundreds of old pioneers of the frontier, and traveled extensively to see at firsthand places dramatically important in the story of the West. Painstaking research was required to show fully and faithfully every facet of Western life he was to portray. Such a background was invaluable for an artist who had made Western life and the Western scene his career.

The magazine feature was very successful and served to make his name known to a larger audience. He established a winter studio in Denver, which he still maintains, and gradually his paintings became sought-after items by galleries in the East and West.

He works with equal facility in oils or water colors. In both mediums his paintings have been awarded many first prizes in important American competitions. Delano's art is exceptional for many qualities: the strong sense of design, the exceptional color, the brilliant quality of light, the accuracy of drawing, and the simplicity of composition.

James E. Swinnerton

Fifty-nine years ago an up-and-coming young newspaper publisher in San Francisco by the name of William Randolph Hearst hired an equally promising young cartoonist by the name of Jimmy Swinnerton to draw for his paper. There was more than a semblance of permanence in the job, because the cartoonist has been with Hearst's King Features Syndicate ever since.

Swinnerton's "Little Jimmy," which appears in most Hearst papers east of the Mississippi, hasn't aged a bit in a half century or so. He and his pup, "Beans," have wormed their way into the affection of millions of readers. The strip is the oldest in existence in United States papers still drawn by the originator. Equally famous are Swinnerton's "Canyon Kiddies," a fascinating group of Indian children whose friends are the gentle creatures of nature. Through this cartoon feature the artist has endeavored to dispel the misinformation that has grown up in the United States about the desert country and its natives. He also tries to initiate his audience, many of them city dwellers, to the beauty and happiness to be found in nature.

Like "Little Jimmy," Jimmy Swinnerton has not aged a bit in a half century, at least not in spirit. His appearance, his wit, and his viewpoint all belie the calendar.

If you want to learn of him, inquire among the Hopis, or the Navajos, or among the lonely ones who operate the trading posts deep in the hills, or in the heart of the desert. He has been painting their country for years and years. He knows all the canyons and he has followed all the faintest trails. This is the country he approaches now with the same

enthusiasm and reverence he felt when he first went into it so many years ago.

A conspicuous success in journalism (he always refers to himself as an old newspaperman), Swinnerton's lasting renown will unquestionably be that of a landscape painter. That he paints, as he says, "for fun," does not make his landscapes any the less attractive. He finds eager buyers for everything that he does now, and his paintings are finding their way into more museums and private collections every day.

James E. Swinnerton was born in Eureka, California, November 13, 1875. His father, who was founder and editor of the Humboldt *Star*, later became a successful lawyer and a judge at Stockton. Swinnerton's mother died a few months after he was born, and during his early boyhood days he lived with his grandparents.

His grandfather had been in the gold rush, a colorful personality who acquired mining property in the Sierras which he later traded for farm lands in the Santa Clara Valley. The elder Swinnerton shared with young Jimmy his love of the Sierra country and his interest in a pioneer era that was passing even before the turn of the century. Grandfather and grandson made quite a pair wandering in the foothills, exploring the valleys, following streams to their sources.

Upon the death of his grandmother, Jimmy went to live with his father, who had remarried. Because he did not enjoy the friendliest of relationships with his stepmother, he ran away at the age of fourteen to San Francisco and became an apprentice harness-racing driver. Jimmy's father, when he finally found

(Text Continued on Page 75)

AVAJOLAND

DESERTED NAVAJO HOME

TER THE SHOWER

MOONRISE—NORTHERN ARIZONA

GRAND CANYON

him and realized his son's determination to go his own way, advised him not to go to college, not to become a lawyer, and by all means not to become a newspaperman. He suggested one of three careers: art, music, or writing. Because he had shown a remarkable talent for drawing, young Jimmy decided to become an artist, and his father enrolled him in the California Art School.

It has not been recorded that any of his instructors found him a particularly promising student. They soon discovered, however, that he had a devilish propensity for caricature, and that too often they, his teachers, appeared as the subjects of his derisive studies. This cartooning talent did not remain long undiscovered.

San Francisco was a young and lively town in those days, and many important developments were having small beginnings. The son of wealthy Senator Hearst was learning the inside and outside of the newspaper game with a newspaper his father had purchased for him—the San Francisco *Examiner*. When Jimmy Swinnerton's drawings were brought to the attention of William Randolph Hearst, Jimmy became a newspaperman. The two formed a friendship that has lasted through the years.

Swinnerton's cartoons, covering sports and news, became popular almost immediately and he was given more and more space in the paper. It might be said that he played an important part in the development of pictorial journalism. Among other ingenious devices, he invented the California weather bear, a type of animated weather forecast, whose antics each day served to predict rain or sunshine, heat or cold.

When Hearst decided to expand into the New York field, Swinnerton went along to contribute to the first Sunday supplement. Swinnerton's "Little Tigers" and "Little Jimmy" were born in the Hearst papers, keeping company with such interesting characters as the "Katzenjammer Kids" and Dick Outcault's "Yellow Kid." In the East the young cartoonist from Eureka found himself in fast company. He was making and spending large sums of money. He lived a gay, full, and fast existence, but it was doomed to be of short duration. While still a very young man, he developed tuberculosis.

When the breakdown came, three consultants held little hope for his recovery and could only recommend a dry climate. In 1903, at the age of twenty-eight, Jimmy Swinnerton, desperately ill, arrived at Palm Springs to begin his struggle for life. Palm Springs was then a desert hamlet consisting of a few tents and barely a handful of people.

The desert with its hot sun gave Jimmy back his health and also gave him his interest in landscape painting. He reacted strongly to the beauty of the new country in which he was forced to live, and since his debt to the desert was so great, it was little wonder he painted it with such deep feeling. Yet when he tried to sell the beauty that he had put on canvas, Eastern critics and collectors said they were not true because they did not conform to the old stereotype of the desert: a wasteland of sand and thorns. But that was long ago.

While he has continued his career as a newspaperman, Swinnerton has never left the desert country. His excursions through the years have taken him farther and farther into the little-known regions of New Mexico, Arizona, and southern Utah. It is in northern Arizona that he has found his greatest inspirations.

He has remained a landscape painter. You can not improve on nature, he says, and nature, without man's interference, is the essence of sublimity. He has taken big subjects for his canvases — mountains, deserts, evening skies—but his talent and skill are of a stature to cope with such bigness.

Ray Strang

Ray Strang lives in the desert near Tucson, Arizona, where desert and foothills meet. He is not a commuting artist who comes out only in the winters to enjoy the sunshine. He lives there all year around, winter and summer, always working, always trying to catch on canvas the subtle, evanescent glimmer of shadow and sunlight that gives the desert its color— or rather, that gives desert colors their life and translucency.

The Arizona desert has, to use an honored cowboy expression, "throwed" many an artist. You just can't grab the Golden State Limited, head West, set up an easel under an umbrella, and slam-bang gaudy colors on canvas. The desert, if you honestly want to capture her moods, requires more skillful wooing.

That Ray Strang has done—and admirably.

He has also come to know the people of the back country of the land in which he lives. Of these people he writes: "It is my job to portray their lives and characters with understanding and enthusiasm. Then some day, when this country is no longer new, it won't matter whether my canvases are dated 1870 or 1950. They will simply be records of the Old West."

Strang was born in Sandoval, Illinois, in 1893. He went to school in Centralia, Illinois, and in 1915 began his studies at the Chicago Art Institute, when that institution was in what has been described as its "Golden Age." His art studies were interrupted by World War I, in which he served and was wounded in the last battle of the Argonne. After the war he returned to the Art Institute, completing his studies there in 1920. He continued his art education in New York at the Art Students League and the Society of Illustrators School.

Artists, like everyone else, have to eat. The roaring twenties, of which Strang found himself a part, was a decade of hurry and bustle and high times when money flowed freely; but unfortunately those who had it to spend professed little interest in the type of pictures Ray Strang wanted to paint. So he became an illustrator, and from the very beginning of his career enjoyed great success.

For seventeen years he was one of America's top illustrators, his work appearing in practically every magazine of consequence in the country. Three large advertising agencies kept him as rushed as the decade in which he lived, and financially he prospered.

In the thirties a chance visit took him to Tucson. That was a turning point in his life because it gave him the inspiration to break from the field of commercial art and do the kind of work he had always wanted to do.

(Text Continued on Page 85)

76

SLOW POKE

SPRING

HORSE POWER

NATIVE'S RETURN

WATER

WAITING FOR MAIL

WOOD GATHERERS

"I might have left with the rest of the 'dudes' that first spring, completely disappointed," he says, "had I not suddenly awakened to the realization that the 'Old West' that I wanted to paint was actually still the West of today. The young men in Levis, big hats and fancy boots that we see on the streets every day are just what they appear to be—cowboys. The cowboy of today is just the same as the cowboy of twenty-five, of fifty, of seventy-five years back. His job hasn't changed a bit. He still makes his living on a horse. Unchanged, too, are those venturesome men who search the mountains and canyons for hidden treasure. The patient, reliable burro still carries the prospector's equipment and shares the lonely trails with him. I discovered the subjects I wanted to paint were of the present as much as the past."

In the desert of southern Arizona, Ray Strang found himself as an artist and discovered that section of America which stirred him the most. His paintings, in a way, are stories expressing the humor, the patience, the loneliness, and the courage of the people of the West. They reveal his intense understanding of the lonely ones who live in the deep canyons and on the arid plains. If you venture back into the hills, away from the wide paved highways, you will meet Ray Strang's people at every turn of the road. They are simple people, and the artist captures the essential dignity of their hard lives.

To know Ray Strang is to understand his paintings. He is a quiet, placid, kindly man, blessed with the eye to see, the heart to understand, and the creative ability to interpret the Western scene so as to strike responsive chords in all of us. His kindliness, his patience, and his good humor shine from his paintings.

By preference as well as by profession he is primarily a figure painter, but the fidelity with which he paints the land in which his people and animals live makes his pictures outstanding. His hills and mesas, his mountains and skies, his desert panoramas have an amazing fidelity. His honesty as a colorist is, perhaps, his greatest concern, his greatest virtue. His scenery does not intrude. It fits in pleasantly with the story he tells. For Ray Strang always has a story to tell.

In his description of "Slow Poke," for instance, he demonstrates a profound understanding of the motives which go into his paintings: "Animals, old and young, have many characteristics that closely parallel what we call human traits. Sometimes they're smart; sometimes they're dumb. They can be stubborn, or willing and lovable. They have their ups and downs just as we do. The little fellow here started out full of beans but now he's tired out. He's too young to realize that there isn't much further to go; he's had enough and is inclined to protest every step. Anyone who has ever taken a scampering youngster or puppy on even a short country hike will recognize the situation. You carry them the rest of the way home."

Ray Strang lives peacefully on sixty acres, with a million miles of colorful country around him. His paintings tell us of his complete fascination with that country.

Gallery of
Western Paintings

Book design by George M. Avey. Produced in
offset lithography by Times-Mirror Press, Los
Angeles, California, under the direct supervision
of Eduard Schroeder. Reproductions herein orig-
inally appeared as art features in the magazine
Arizona Highways. The editor and publisher express thanks to the various artists who cooperated
in making their paintings available; to Edith
Hamblin Dixon for the paintings by Maynard
Dixon; to Homer E. Britzman for the paintings
by Charles M. Russell; to the Frederic Remington
Estate and Remington Art Memorial, Ogdens-
burg, N. Y., and the Valley National Bank,
Phoenix, Arizona, for the paintings of Frederic
Remington.